WAL

ARNSIDE &
SILVERDALE

HILLSIDE GUIDES - ACROSS THE NORTH

Long Distance Walks
•COAST TO COAST WALK   •DALES WAY   •CUMBRIA WAY
•WESTMORLAND WAY •FURNESS WAY •LADY ANNE'S WAY •PENDLE WAY
•BRONTE WAY   •CALDERDALE WAY   •NIDDERDALE WAY

Circular Walks - Yorkshire Dales
•WHARFEDALE   •MALHAMDALE   •SWALEDALE   •NIDDERDALE
•THREE PEAKS   •WENSLEYDALE   •HOWGILL FELLS
•HARROGATE & WHARFE VALLEY   •RIPON & LOWER WENSLEYDALE

Hillwalking - Lake District
•LAKELAND FELLS - SOUTH   •LAKELAND FELLS - EAST
•LAKELAND FELLS - NORTH   •LAKELAND FELLS - WEST

Circular Walks - Lancashire/Cumbria
•BOWLAND   •PENDLE & THE RIBBLE   •WEST PENNINE MOORS
•ARNSIDE & SILVERDALE   •LUNESDALE

Circular Walks - North Pennines
•TEESDALE   •EDEN VALLEY   •ALSTON & ALLENDALE

Circular Walks - North East Yorkshire
•NORTH YORK MOORS, SOUTHERN   •HOWARDIAN HILLS

Circular Walks - South Pennines
•ILKLEY MOOR   •BRONTE COUNTRY
•CALDERDALE   •SOUTHERN PENNINES

Short Scenic Walks - Full Colour Pocket Guides
Yorkshire Dales
•UPPER WHARFEDALE   •LOWER WHARFEDALE   •MALHAMDALE
•UPPER WENSLEYDALE   •LOWER WENSLEYDALE   •SWALEDALE
•NIDDERDALE   •SEDBERGH & DENTDALE
•RIBBLESDALE   •INGLETON & WESTERN DALES
Northern England
•HARROGATE & KNARESBOROUGH   •ILKLEY & WASHBURN VALLEY
•AIRE VALLEY   •AMBLESIDE & LANGDALE   •BORROWDALE
•BOWLAND   •AROUND PENDLE   •RIBBLE VALLEY

*Send for a detailed current catalogue and price list
and also visit www.hillsidepublications.co.uk*

WALKING COUNTRY

ARNSIDE &
SILVERDALE

Paul Hannon

Hillside

HILLSIDE
PUBLICATIONS
20 Wheathead Crescent
Keighley
West Yorkshire
BD22 6LX

First published 2007
2nd impression 2010

ISBN 978-1-870141-84-0

To Lisa,
Remembering our first walk on that special spring weekend

Cover illustration: The Kent Estuary from Arnside Knott
Back cover: White Creek; Lancaster Canal; Hutton Roof Crags
Page One: The Pepper Pot, Castlebarrow, Silverdale
Page Three: Swan and cygnets, Lancaster Canal
(Paul Hannon/Hillslides Picture Library)

The sketch maps in this book are based upon
1947 Ordnance Survey One-Inch maps

Printed in Great Britain by
Carnmor Print
95-97 London Road
Preston
Lancashire
PR1 4BA

CONTENTS

INTRODUCTION

Located between Lancaster in North Lancashire and Kendal in South Cumbria, the Arnside & Silverdale Area of Outstanding Natural Beauty was designated as such in 1972, and comprising a mere 29 square miles it is one of the smallest in the country. Occupying a seemingly secretive setting where the Kent Estuary opens out into Morecambe Bay, this is a delightful world of limestone features and rich woodland. Add to these natural charms some lovely villages, magnificent houses such as Leighton Hall, Dallam Tower and Borwick Hall; fortified pele towers at Arnside, Beetham and Hazelslack; some invaluable marshes of which Leighton Moss is a long established and internationally important bird reserve; and beautiful views over the estuary to the Lakeland Fells, also inland to the Three Peaks country of Yorkshire.

This gorgeous tract of land is typified by the absorbing tangle of limestone outcrops and walls, lush pastures, mixed woodland and fascinating seashore. Immediately across the motorway is a very different yet logically linked landscape, that of the more open, less wooded and less populated limestone heights of Hutton Roof and Farleton. That these were not also included in the area of protection is laughable, their case is equally worthy: this guide, at least, treats them as equals. Also included is a man-made corridor that runs between the two areas, not the pulsating M6 but the contrastingly leisurely sweep of the Lancaster Canal, an almost forgotten waterway whose towpath is a delight to tread.

A great bonus of accessibility is the location of M6 junctions 35 and 36, and the Furness rail line which turns off from Carnforth and offers ideally sited stations at Silverdale and Arnside.

Access to the countryside

The majority of walks in this guide are on public rights of way with no access restrictions, or long-established access areas and paths. Some also take advantage of the 2004 implementation of 'Right to Roam', allowing more logical routes to be created: such walks are noted in their introduction. Existing access areas and concession paths now largely fall within this Open Country, and on most days of the year you are free to walk responsibly over these wonderful landscapes. Further information can be obtained from the Countryside Agency, and ideally from information centres.

Using the guide
    Each walk is self-contained, with essential information being followed by a concise route description and simple map. Dovetailed in between are notes and illustrations of features along the way. Snippets of information have been placed in *italics* to ensure that the essential route description is easier to locate. The sketch maps serve to identify the location of the routes rather than the fine detail, and whilst the description should be sufficient to guide you around, an Ordnance Survey map is strongly recommended.
    To gain the most from a walk, the detail of the 1:25,000 scale Explorer map is unsurpassed. It also gives the option to vary walks as desired, giving an improved picture of your surroundings and the availability of linking paths. Just one map covers all the walks:
• *Explorer OL7 - English Lakes South East*
Also useful for planning is Landranger map 97 (scale 1:50,000)

USEFUL ADDRESSES

Ramblers' Association
2nd Floor, Camelford House, 87-89 Albert Embankment, London SE1 7BR
• 020-7339 8500
Arnside & Silverdale AONB
The Old Station Building, Arnside LA5 0HG   • 01524-761034
Tourist Information Centres
29 Castle Hill **Lancaster** LA1 1YN • 01524-32878
Town Hall, Highgate **Kendal** LA9 4DL • 01539-725758
Victoria Hall, Main St **Grange-over-Sands** LA11 6DP • 015395-34026
Cumbria Tourist Board
Ashleigh, Holly Road, Windermere LA23 2AQ • 015394-44444
Lancashire & Blackpool Tourist Board
St George's House, St George's St, Chorley PR7 2AA • 01257-226600
Leighton Moss RSPB Nature Reserve
Myers Farm, Silverdale, Carnforth LA5 0SW • 01524-701601
British Waterways Lancaster Office
Main Road, Galgate, Lancaster LA2 0LQ • 01524-751888
Open Access
Helpline • 0845-100 3298, *or* www.countrysideaccess.gov.uk
Public Transport Information
Traveline • 0870 608 2608 National Rail Enquiries • 08457-484950

DALLAM PARK & BEETHAM

START *Milnthorpe*   *Grid ref. SD 497814*

DISTANCE *5³⁄4 miles (9km)*

ORDNANCE SURVEY MAPS
1:50,000
Landranger 97 - Kendal & Morecambe
1:25,000
Explorer OL7 - English Lakes South East

ACCESS *Start from the crossroads in the village centre. Parking in the adjacent square, with a car park on Park Road west from the crossroads. Served by bus from Kendal and Lancaster.*

> *Richly contrasting rambling from the lovely parkland of Dallam to glorious woodland and inner estuary views*

Milnthorpe is a typical grey-stone Westmorland village that is a lively focal point of local life. 200 years ago numerous mills operated here, and the arrival of the Lancaster-Kendal turnpike brought trade that remains to this day on the busy A6. The market square still supports a Friday market, and adjoining it the church of St Thomas dates from 1837. The striking Roman Catholic church of Christ the King hides behind nearby houses. Within a stone's throw of the market cross are several pubs, shops, a café and WC.

From the central crossroads head west on the B5782 Arnside road, and on the edge of the village a stone-arched bridge crosses the River Bela into Dallam Park. This marks a rapid transformation into a scene of great beauty, with the house set back beyond the river. *Dallam Tower began life as a pele tower, but since the early 18th century has been a stately mansion. The Bela flows gracefully through the park, less than a mile before its entry into the Kent.*

The walk will return to this spot, so forsake the river and aim directly up the slope ahead, passing right of the main brow. *Savour great views of the house in its stately setting, and north over the inner Kent estuary and up the Lyth Valley to the Lakeland Fells.*

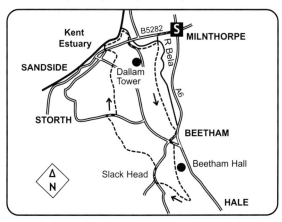

Across a dip head up a second brow. *During this pull look back left to see the deer house, with the resident herd of Fallow deer often close by.* Just left of the very brow the park is left by a little bridge over a ha-ha, and Beetham now appears ahead. *Principal feature is its extensive paper works.* Descend between a new avenue of trees to a stile/gate onto an access road at Heron Corn Mill. *The restored mill dates from about 1750, but on a much older site, and is now a paper-making museum. A water-powered wheel operates and visitors can witness the milling process.*

Advance straight along this road into Beetham, bearing right for the village centre. *Beetham is a tiny grey-stone village stood happily clear of the busy A6. Of several old buildings the rambling Wheatsheaf Hotel is a welcoming spot, with a small Post office close by. Pride of place goes to the ancient church of St Michael, whose relative size is due to its past importance. The tower dates back eight centuries, and its strangely narrow structure appears out of proportion. Also based here in a former chapel is the Heron Theatre, home of the South Westmorland Stage & Screen Society.*

Bear left along the front of the pub to another junction and left again, briefly, to where a footpath turns off right before a short row of houses. It runs along the back gardens and out into a field. Cross diagonally towards Beetham Hall farm (some field boundaries have disappeared here), bearing further right of the wall end. A stile sends a path along the base of a wood, with good views of the pele tower. *The crumbling pele at Beetham Hall is typical of several in the area, built as defence against marauding Scots in the 14th century.* At the end continue the length of the pasture alongside an attractive limestone scar. On the edge of Hale at the far end, ignore the stile in front and bear right, up a track at the wood corner and an enclosed path runs on above a garden and up through a stile into the woods proper. *Just off-route, Hale has the Kings Arms pub and the Lakeland Wildlife Oasis.*

Within half a minute you reach a T-junction at a wall corner: watch all the waymarks for the next half-mile, potential confusion awaits! Go straight across a crossroads just beyond, and just yards further is a fork at the base of a limestone scar. Bear right on this, up the scar and join a wall on the right, on through a wonderland of lichen-covered outcrops and scattered birch. Immediately go straight over another crossroads with a level path, and continue rising by the wall, now as a thinner path. Rise to pass through a gap at a wall junction, and the now level path bears a little left, soon reaching a fork: turn sharp right, broader again and still level.

The way remains broad, level and clear beneath conifers, but before long forks into two lesser branches. Go left to quickly reach a broader path. Turn right two yards to a waymark, then strike off unconvincingly left, immediately onto a gem of a limestone pavement that tilts away: cross at an angle to emerge into a clearing on this splendid, dead-flat pavement. Towards the bottom corner drop a little more directly left, back into undergrowth and gently down with the big clearing of Deepdale to the right. The path runs to a fork where go straight on, bearing right with the road visible just ahead. The way proper swings right just yards from the end, for a winding little finish through scrub out onto the road.

Turn right, gently rising to a junction at the scattered houses of Slack Head. Go straight on as the road starts to descend. Part way down take a rough road alongside a short row of houses. Follow it right at the end then keep straight on the continuing path, past a final cottage and into the wood proper. This same path now rises a little to run pleasantly on through trees. An appreciable limestone scar forms up to the left, to eventually reach a junction marked by a cairn. While the main paths go left and right, advance straight on a thinner one, past the wall-end on the left, then more faintly up through low outcrops to meet a wall on the right.

St Michael's church, Beetham

Ignore a small gate in the wall to rise to pass through a stile just above, then the clearer path rises a very short way to join a broad path alongside a wall gateway. Turn right, away, at once into a splendid clearing on the brow of Beetham Fell. This broad path runs on the edge of this linear clearing to another marker cairn. This time remain on the main path straight on, soon back into denser woodland. Running an unmistakable course, you gradually descend to be joined by a wall from the right to run on to emerge onto the brow of another road through the woods.

Turn right briefly, and escape left at the first opportunity into more woodland on the left. Two paths head away, take the broad one straight ahead. This nice way soon reaches a T-junction, where go right to drop down to a junction with a broader path. Go left, commencing a sustained pull on a broad limestone track, rising to a covered reservoir on the top of Haverbrack. From a kissing-gate just beyond, a field is entered with the great spread of the estuary and South Lakeland to the north. Head down the field alongside a sturdy limestone wall, savouring this glorious prospect.

At the bottom corner a narrow back road is joined. Straight across, a stile sends a path down the side of a wood. At the very bottom, as path and wall swing left, the true path faintly slants down to the right, locating Hollins Well hidden at the bottom wall. A thin path then runs left along the wood bottom to rejoin the main one to leave the wood. A broad track then drops down onto the B5282 Arnside road. Go left 100 yards and cross to steps sending a path down onto the old rail embankment, immediately above the foreshore. Shortly it vacates the bank and drops down to the very foreshore, following this round for a lovely if brief coastal section of the walk. Rounding a limestone point, the River Bela directs you back inland, tracing it past a weir back to the road.

Note the rail embankment's abrupt termination in the field alongside: the 26-arch viaduct across the Bela was demolished in 1963 after closure of the Arnside-Sandside-Hincaster link. Cross over to follow the public road past the lodge of 1881 into Dallam Park. A kissing-gate admits to the riverbank, which is followed the short way back to the Bela bridge to retrace outward steps.

The Fairy Steps

THE FAIRY STEPS

START Sandside   Grid ref. SD 475807

DISTANCE 3³₄ miles (6km)

ORDNANCE SURVEY MAPS
1:50,000
Landranger 97 - Kendal & Morecambe
1:25,000
Explorer OL7 - English Lakes South East

ACCESS Start from the B5282 coast road in the village. Ample parking beyond the Ship Inn (Arnside direction) on the broad road. Served by Arnside-Kendal bus via Milnthorpe.

> A coastal start leads into delightful woodland with limestone features crowned by the dramatic cleft of the Fairy Steps

Sandside is a small village with an aptly descriptive name, protruding out into Milnthorpe Sands in the Kent Estuary. Focal point is the Ship Inn, while the village had its own station on the line between Arnside and Milnthorpe. Before even starting, take time to appraise a view that is quite astonishing, given this sea level location. Across the big tides and beyond the great bulk of nearby Whitbarrow is an array of Lakeland fells that include Coniston Old Man, the Langdale Pikes, Ill Bell and High Street, while further east are the Whinfell Ridge and the Howgill Fells. A refreshment van may be in evidence at the start.

Head east on the footway, which ends as you might briefly use the grassy foreshore before returning to the Ship Inn. Past its car park a path takes a short snicket onto a parallel back road. It also crosses the old railway on the edge of Sandside Cutting. Turn left on the road then double back right up a rough road. This zigzags up through scrub outside Sandside Quarry on your left. After a second branch left into the quarry edge, escape straight ahead on a broad, level path into trees. This runs pleasantly on to a T-junction of paths with an open pasture just ahead. Turn right, almost at once becoming an access lane out past cottages on the edge of Storth.

At the end of the pasture turn off at a stile on the left, and a path runs along the wood edge and into the trees. *Just before entering, a nice cameo is presented by the distant but ever shapely Langdale Pikes appearing through a gap.* The path now rises past a limestone edge to the right, then undertakes a delightful ramble through this wonderland. Ignoring any lesser branches you reach a T-junction of like paths just a minute short of a gap-stile onto a road through the woods.

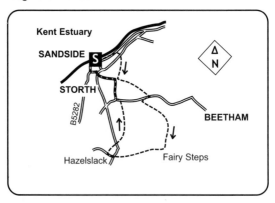

Double back right briefly, to the brow, and take a broad path doubling back to the left. This runs an unmistakable course as it rises straight and true, very gently with a wall and then fencing. On your right is a lichen-covered limestone pavement. Eventually the path emerges to level out at the edge of a linear clearing on the brow of Beetham Fell. Advance just as far as a four-way marker cairn. Take the grassy path bearing gently right, along the clearing edge to plunge back into undergrowth. This path runs a splendid level course, with a substantial limestone cliff forming on the left.

Simply remain on this path to arrive at a junction with a descending path. While the continuation is to the right, first go left for a matter of a few steps to find yourself at the foot of the cliff, and with it the hidden Fairy Steps. The 'steps' are a narrow cleft in the limestone cliff, and something of a 'fat man's agony'. Even though technically off-route it would be folly to omit them, so ease your way up to earn a relaxing sojourn on the open ground above. *The delectable clearing atop the cliff also brings the walk's great views, with the southern fells of Lakeland seen over the treetops. The route was used in the past as a coffin route to Beetham church, and also, of course, by the fairies!*

Resuming, descend the cleft and head down the clear path. A lesser version of the Fairy Steps is quickly encountered, the path this time sloping down behind the lower tier of limestone. A direct descent through Underlaid Wood ensues, passing another modest lichen-covered pavement. Emerging from the wood, a green track runs along the fieldsides to a road junction at Hazelslack Tower Farm. Cross straight over and along the road between the farm buildings. *Dominating the farm is a ruined pele tower, which despite its condition and the mellowing effect of its foliage still looks mightily impressive. Like others in the vicinity it was built in the late 14th century to afford protection from marauding Scots.* Just beyond, take a stile on the right and head past the foot of the tower to a wall-stile beyond. Now make for the far end of the larger, hummocky pasture to a stile onto a narrow road.

Cross to a stile opposite and follow a track away. As it swings right to become enclosed by walls, bear left to an interesting stile fronted with stone steps in the wall corner. Now simply follow the wall on the left beneath a wooded bank and limestone scar hidden in trees up to the left. Almost entirely enclosed by woodland, you eventually reach a stile into the woods at the far end, from where a rough, stony track rises to a gate. Back into daylight, follow the wall on the left again, through a field surrounded by woodland. A stile at the far end deposits you onto Cockshot Lane.

Turn left just as far as a junction, then fork right beneath a limestone scar on Throughs Lane, through woodland to enter the top corner of Storth. Bear left on the road into the village and down to a junction by the Post office/shop. Cross straight over onto a little triangular green with a war memorial and resume down Green Lane, over the railway cutting and down onto the coast road at Sandside. Turn right to finish.

HAWES WATER

START *Arnside   Grid ref. SD 456788*

DISTANCE *6^{1}2 miles (10^{1}2km)*

ORDNANCE SURVEY MAPS
1:50,000
Landranger 97 - Kendal & Morecambe
1:25,000
Explorer OL7 - English Lakes South East

ACCESS *Start from the tiny pier on the front. Roadside parking, and a car park on the shore. Served by bus from Kendal, by Sunday bus from Carnforth, and by Carnforth-Barrow trains.*

> *A visit to a secluded tarn hidden amid the gentle limestone pastures of Gait Barrows nature reserve*

For a note on Arnside, see page 20. Follow the road out past the station, keeping straight on Black Dyke Road at the junction. Head on through suburbia to a junction, where turn left down a short-lived lane to the railway line. Across, an enclosed path runs on across the fields of Arnside Moss. *Here, at 6am one spring morning, a large fox strode bold as brass alongside me. Ahead are the woodlands secreting the Fairy Steps.* On crossing a second drain you emerge into an open pasture. *Look back through the gap to the houses of Arnside sheltering beneath the wooded Arnside Knott.* Keep straight on a thin path that runs through a hedgerow towards the end and along to a corner stile onto a back road.

Cross straight over to another gap-stile and across a small field, through small limestone outcrops towards a gate at the far end. Ignoring this, use a gap-stile in the wall on the right. Turn left a few yards to another stile by a gate. Through it go forward to join a farm track which is followed to the far end of the field (an occasional caravan site). Joining a narrow road, turn right past Hazelslack Tower Farm to a T-junction. *Dominating the farm is a ruined pele tower, which despite its condition and the mellowing effect of its foliage still looks mightily impressive. Like others in the vicinity it dates from the late 14th century, built to afford protection from marauding Scots.*

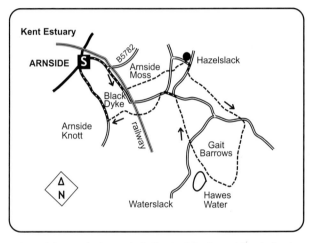

Turn right again here, briefly, before branching left along a hedgerowed cart track. This winds pleasantly along and is left at a signed path from a gate on the right, as the nearby trees end. Cross the field to find a plank bridge close to a lone tree, then turn left with the syke before bearing right through a gateway ahead. Continue along a wallside, and at the end the faint path surmounts the gentlest of brows to pass through another gateway. Again resume with a wall, at the end a firm track forming to lead out to a gate onto a road at Leighton Beck Bridge.

Advance the short way to the junction at the stone arched bridge and take a stile on the right. Rise up the field and cross to a gap in the hedgerow ahead, colonising a distinctive limestone outcropping band. Continue straight on to a clump of trees, behind which are fence and wall stiles. Advance further towards a wall corner enclosing a wood, with a distinctive limestone arrangement (a modest 'Devil's Bowling Green') in front. Pass through this and head away with the wall to find a stile in a facing wall. Continue over the brow, island-like amid a woodland surround, and on to a fence-stile in the corner.

Go right a few yards then bear left on a thin path down through a clearing in the trees. As this quickly forks, bear right through a line of trees and maintain this course down towards a wall corner. Bear right close by the wall and on through a stile by a fenced woodland enclosure. The path then drops down onto an enclosed green way. Take the gap-stile in the wall in front and bear right to a path crossroads at a stile in another wall close by West Coppice.

Pass through the gate into Gait Barrows National Nature Reserve. *A panel advises that this is one of the finest limestone pavements in Britain, along with ancient yew woodlands and important wetlands around Hawes Water.* The faintest of paths bears left across the flower-rich pasture, passing through an old wall and down to a kissing-gate in the bottom corner. Here a clear path is met in the woodland fringing Hawes Water. Turn right, with an early chance to take a closer look at the shore on a permissive path. Resuming, the path broadens as it leaves the tarn behind. When it swings sharp left, now between old walls, instead take the broad path branching through a gateway on the right. This ascends to run on through woodland to emerge via a stile onto a road.

Cross straight over and resume on a broad path into Challan Hall Wood. This ends at a gate, where cross a small enclosure and continue on a part enclosed old way. At the end a twin-slab foot-bridge crosses tiny Leighton Beck. *This is not into woodland as the map suggests, but a very open pasture. Across to the left Arnside Tower stands silhouetted in the dip between Middlebarrow and Arnside Knott, an impressive scene.* Now bear left to a gate/stile above a tinier stream, then rise right between two walled woods. Beyond the island wood on the left bear left to cross to a stile/gate onto a road.

Turn left and keep left at successive junctions. After the second leave the road at a stile opposite Moss Dyke Farm. Bear right across a curious ditch with low outcrops to join a farm track. Bear left on this to swing round to an underpass below the railway. Through it stands a venerable and informative old footpath sign, where turn right to a corner stile. Sandwiched between trees and railway embankment, a path runs on to emerge into a small field. Advance between modern barns onto a farm road just short of the road at Black Dyke level crossing. *If desperate to finish, turn right onto the road, and then left up Briery Bank.*

Without setting foot on the road, turn sharp left into Hagg Wood. A good path climbs the woodside to enter modern suburbia. Go right of the first house then rise between houses onto Spinney Lane, which joins Silverdale Road. Turn right along this suburban road and keep left at the end by Our Lady of Lourdes Roman Catholic church. *Here you can enjoy good views over rolling hills to the flat top of Ingleborough just visible over the much closer Hutton Roof Crags, with Lakeland's Far Eastern fells seen over the estuary.* Advancing into the village, descend at the end to reach the front at the Albion pub. Alternatively, as you start descending locate a gate on the left, set back, from where a permissive path winds down through Ashmeadow woodlands to reach the front at the road-end.

Hazelslack Tower

19

4

ARNSIDE KNOTT

START Arnside   Grid ref. SD 456788

DISTANCE $5^1⁄4$ miles ($8^1⁄2$km)

ORDNANCE SURVEY MAPS
1:50,000
Landranger 97 - Kendal & Morecambe
1:25,000
Explorer OL7 - English Lakes South East

ACCESS Start from the tiny pier. Roadside parking, and a car park on the shore. Served by bus from Kendal, by Sunday bus from Carnforth, and by train from Carnforth and Barrow.

> *A beautiful walk of two halves, with a super coastal ramble leading to a gentle ascent of the area's finest viewpoint*

Arnside is no standard seaside resort, for its attractions, other than natural, are strictly limited. A couple of pubs (the Albion and the Fighting Cocks) and a number of shops and cafes are strung along the seafront. Despite a healthy number of visitors Arnside remains essentially residential, and behind its waterfront sprawls a relatively vast hinterland of modern suburbia. Just out in the bay, the Lake District National Park reaches its most southerly point between here and Grange-over-Sands, which is three miles distant (as the crow flies) and clearly visible.

A bright and breezy place, Arnside stands at the point where the Kent Estuary gives way to the waters of Morecambe Bay, the massive Kent Viaduct proving an arbitrary border. Trains pulling out of Arnside station are on it within seconds, heading for Furness. This impressive monument to the railway engineers was completed in 1857, and boasts no less than 50 arches. The

Ulverston & Lancaster Railway Company constructed a wharf for shipping that could no longer reach Milnthorpe after the viaduct was built. Today's modest surviving pier was restored after being ripped apart by storms in the winter of 1981-82. Arnside is also headquarters of the AONB, based in an old station building.

Important: signs warning of fast rising tides, quicksands and hidden channels are not there for fun. The speed of some of the incoming tides has to be seen to be believed. Under absolutely no circumstances should you wander aimlessly out onto sandbanks without knowledge or awareness of tide times.

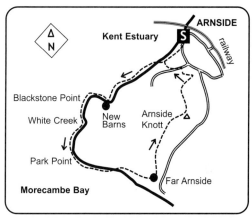

From the Promenade follow the road south - with the estuary on your right - to its abrupt terminus (or ideally follow the shore-line). At the end a concrete path takes over, above the part rocky shore and beneath woodland. This remains the format for much of the way. The Beach Walk Cafe and Coastguard station are quickly reached, beyond which the path clings to the shoreline, with its outcropping limestone, to approach the creek at New Barns Bay. Having sunk into oozing sand up to the knees, it can be confirmed that crossing the main creek may have its pitfalls: recommended is the path along the wood edge to bridge the stream and thus join an access road. Follow this right to rejoin the shore path at the house at New Barns.

A super walk leads around to Blackstone Point, ideally on the broad sands beneath shoreline cliffs. If high tides negate this, take the woodland path from New Barns to White Creek, where one can then use the clifftop path. The gentle arc of a modest bay at White Creek is then encountered. At low water it is simply a matter of striding out on the firm sands to Arnside Point, though one has the option - or the necessity, at high tide - to follow the shingle bank past a caravan site hidden just yards inland. Across these stones a small path enters the trees to find a broader one through a gateway in an old wall. Turning right on this, it sets about a march along the crest of the largely unbroken cliffs that take over. With caution at the occasional exposed moment, this is a magical section.

From Arnside Point to the rocky spit of Park Point and then swinging back east to reveal the Silverdale shoreline, this is all smashing stuff. The beach below encounters a stony and sometimes rocky shoreline, and with the channel hard by, there is little option but to clamber over the rocks. The path in the trees rises through woodland to meet another path, then resumes to suddenly enter a static caravan park. Follow the upper road that heads away, and remain on this through the exclusive site to emerge at Far Arnside.

Leaving the site advance just a short way along the lane, then a stile on the left sends a fieldpath rising to the farm at Hollins. A stile admits onto its drive, but turn immediately left past the barns, through a gate and up an enclosed little way to a gate admitting to the extensive open pasture of Heathwaite. Turn sharp right on the broad path rising alongside a wall, initially. This ascends in increasing style to the top, where a path crossroads is met on the slopes of Arnside Knott.

Cross straight over the bridlepath (known as Saul's Drive) and continue ascending on a good path, through more open slopes as a broad track climbing to a seat. *Pause here to look back over the expansive woodland of Arnside Park, around which you traced the coastline to Far Arnside*. The climb resumes and eventually eases to run on a narrower spine passing a seat on the right that enjoys a fine view down to the Silverdale shoreline. Easy going continues past the forlorn remains of a knotted larch tree. *This celebrated landmark was one of two created by Victorian visitors, possibly as a love symbol. Just beyond is another fine viewpoint seat, where the broad track fades.*

Just up to the right a thin path runs to the OS column at 521ft/159m crowning Arnside Knott. *This rounded limestone hill is cloaked on three sides by woodland and is a sentinel watching over the estuary. Though its flat top is screened by trees and scrub, fear not as the Knott's delights as a viewpoint will quickly be revealed. Much of it is in the hands of the National Trust.*

The main path resumes by swinging left into scattered trees and quickly merges with a wall from the left. Just yards further is a rustic kissing-gate giving access to exquisite and vast open slopes. *This class moment gives the anticipated view: highlight of this far-reaching panorama is the map-like scene at your feet, with the Kent Viaduct and the houses of Arnside appearing like models. Beyond is a stupendous array of Lakeland fells overtopping the myriad delights of South Lakeland.* Descending the centre is a broad green path, a gem that gives time to savour this classic view.

At the bottom corner a kissing-gate enters woodland, and a path runs down to High Knott Road serving exclusive residences. Turn left and double back right down it to meet another road. For a quicker finish turn right on this to the through road in the village, then left down to the front by the Albion. Preferably though, take the road left, looking out for a public footpath along a private road on the right which runs on and down to end at the last house. Here a footpath drops right down a wood side to suddenly emerge at the Beach Walk Cafe. Retrace the opening few steps to finish.

The coastal path at Arnside Point

STATION TO STATION

START Silverdale Grid ref. SD 476751

FINISH Arnside

DISTANCE 4¹4 miles (7km)

ORDNANCE SURVEY MAPS
1:50,000
Landranger 97 - Kendal & Morecambe
1:25,000
Explorer OL7 - English Lakes South East

ACCESS Start from Silverdale railway station and finish at Arnside station. If coming by car, park at Arnside and catch the train to Silverdale. Both stations are on the Carnforth-Barrow line.

> A linear walk through the heart of the area, with a splendid old pele tower among many fine features

From the station turn right on Red Bridge Lane, then take a stile on the left onto a corner of the golf course. The path is marked by large yellow discs: ascend the woodside and over a brow, across a fairway and up a bank. Across another fairway rise to a kissing-gate onto a road. Turn right, dropping down to the start of the line of houses at The Row. At a bend take a gate on the left and follow a fieldside path away. Over to the right is the expanse of Eaves Wood. From a kissing-gate at the end cross the field centre, soon spotting a squeezer-stile in the wall ahead. The church tower is also in sight. Follow the wallside away, left, to a gate onto Bottoms Lane.

Go right a very short way to a gate on the left. Walk a few paces around the outside of the wood to a gateway, then bear right on the nearside of the wall striking across the field. Further on a kissing-gate transfers to the other side. The Pepper Pot on Castlebarrow is upstanding at the top of Eaves Wood. Resume to a gap-stile in the corner, from where a snicket runs past gardens to emerge at a driveway junction. Turn right on a track past a house and out onto a road just past the church. *St John's has a solid tower that is focal point for scattered Silverdale. The village centre is just back along the road to the left. Here are the Silverdale and the Royal hotels, along with a Post office, shops, WC, and a fine Millennium clock.*

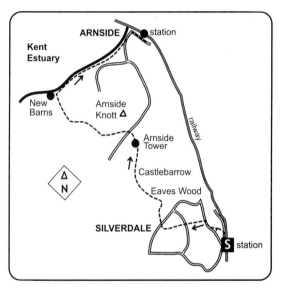

Turn right thirty paces and leave by a snicket between houses on the left, running splendidly along to Cove Road. Turn right to a bend, then advance straight on Elmslack Lane, which swings left to climb to the base of Eaves Wood. *This delightful wood is in the care of the National Trust.* Entering by the gateway you have a choice of routes. The direct one continues straight up the private road, and at the top a path bears right along a garden edge to a stile into the wood. Head on through trees, rising very gently to another stile in a cross-wall and on through coppiced woodland.

The Castlebarrow option leaves the firm road at the gateway to double back right on a wood-bottom path. Within 75 paces, just as it is about to enter a dark walled section, a path climbs left to a clearing beneath a magnificent, gnarled old beech tree. *Backed by a modest limestone ledge, a good dozen main trunks spread from within three feet of the ground.* The path turns right beneath the trees then turns to rise left, on and up to a fork of thinner branches. Turn right, quickly reaching a T-junction with a broad, level path. With a gateway in a wall just to the right, instead turn left, through a part clearing. Now gently rising to a fork, bear left to slant up a small wooded bank to the crest of Castlebarrow.

The landmark Pepper Pot monument was erected in 1887 to commemorate the Golden Jubilee of Queen Victoria. This stunning viewpoint offers a superb contrast between the wooded and coastal delights of the Silverdale scene outspread below, and the inland heights of Ingleborough and Bowland. A limestone pavement sits on the crest. Leave by returning to the broader path just down the small bank, then turn left along a path which runs to a sturdy wall. Turn left with this, descending to a wall junction gateway, and just a minute further down the direct route is joined at a stile.

ROUTES MERGE: Through the stile head away on a good path. A caravan site is seen through the trees on the left. At a fork slant gently left to run grandly on to suddenly emerge at the far point of the site, by a play area at Middlebarrow Plain. Maintaining the same line, join the tarmac road and head briefly along the 'no entry' section to quickly see a waymark sending the invisible path left over the grass. Within yards a very clear path forms to resume as if nothing had changed. *Ahead are the distinctive Shilla Slopes, steep limestone screes on the flank of Arnside Knott.*

The path drops gently through scrub to very quickly witness the dramatic appearance of Arnside Tower. Cross the ladder-stile and along the path left of the ruin down to the modern farm of the same name. *Arnside Tower is one of a number of pele towers built in the area to afford defence against marauding Scots. This largely well-preserved example dates from the 14th century.* Pass through the gate left of the house into the yard and up the drive onto the Silverdale-Arnside road. *At this point take a last look back at the impressive pele beneath the extensive woodland of Middlebarrow Hill, and also across to the limestone heights of Farleton Fell.*

Cross straight over to a bridle-gate onto the flanks of Arnside Knott. The broad track of Saul's Drive slants very gently up to the left, remain on this as it ascends to a gate and a crossroads with a path, with the open country of Heathwaite to the left. *An option here is to transfer to the Knott's ascent path on WALK 4.* Keep straight on over the path's brow, dropping gently right and along to a gate in a sturdy wall. While the bridleway runs straight on, your way is the path left, alongside the wall. When the wall quickly turns left, your broad path turns right, emerging into delectable open country. *The surroundings of scattered trees, scrub and bracken are further enhanced by views ahead over the estuary.*

Remain on this super path as it drops into trees and a gate in a wall. The grand path continues straight down through Copridding Wood to exit via a ladder-stile. An enclosed path heads off between fields to a kissing-gate onto a narrow road. Turn briefly left until it emerges onto the edge of New Barns Bay, a super moment. While the road runs on to serve the cottage, your way is the path along the edge of the marsh to the right. At the rocky point at the end a path rises right into trees and along to stile to follow the field above the edge, but the finest way, tides permitting, is to remain on the beach and follow the part stony shore (or sand) around the point, with the viaduct appearing ahead, and the way becoming firmer as you approach the Coastguard station and adjacent cafe. The path is now surfaced for the final stage running delightfully on into Arnside. For the station, simply remain along the front.

Arnside Tower

JENNY BROWN'S POINT

START *Silverdale Grid ref. SD 471759*

DISTANCE *5$\frac{1}{4}$ miles (8$\frac{1}{2}$km)*

ORDNANCE SURVEY MAPS
1:50,000
Landranger 97 - Kendal & Morecambe
1:25,000
Explorer OL7 - English Lakes South East

ACCESS *Start from the National Trust's Eaves Wood car park, between the village centre and the station. Served by bus linking village and station. The station is on the Carnforth-Barrow line.*

A richly varied exploration of the Silverdale scene, with superb coastal and woodland paths linking the village's scattered corners

From the car park rejoin the road and head directly away along the narrow side road, The Row. Part way along the line of houses look out for a gap on the left, where an enclosed path runs between gardens. At the end a small gate puts you into woodland. Head away, keeping right, and the path drops to a fence-stile before turning sharp right. It runs on through an increasingly attractive, intriguing trough, passing an old iron water pump at Dogslack Well. Just beyond, a cart track takes over to lead out through trees onto a road. Turn left very briefly then take an enclosed path by the side of a lone house on the right. Entering woodland it soon drops down some steps and along to a small gate out into Lambert's Meadow. *This National Trust land is a preserved island of green, damp meadowland.*

Cross the centre to a footbridge, then go left with the stream to a corner kissing-gate back into trees: source of the stream is

Burton Well, to your left. A broad path heads away beneath size-able limestone cliffs, rising gently and at the end swinging sharp right along the wood edge. Emerging at Burtonwell Cottage, its short drive runs on to join Bottoms Lane at The Green (Sunday name Silverdale Green). Turn left to a T-junction and left again. After a short while take a kissing-gate on the right into Clark's Lot. *This is a National Trust permissive area.* Head away on a gentle grass track, into a clearing with limestone around, swinging right in front of trees. Don't continue to the tapering end, but remain on the grassy way and bear left to a gate into trees.

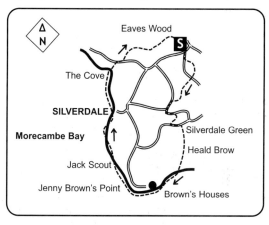

A path heads away, quickly meeting a wall and following it right to a corner. Here go left to a gate out of the trees and down the fieldside to a gate onto another road, Hollins Lane. Go left for a few minutes into more open surrounds, until a path heads off at the start of woodland on the right. The path runs along the edge of Fleagarth Wood and into trees to emerge at the end by intriguing tilted limestone slabs. *This is a glorious moment as you overlook the embankment area, Warton Crag woods, Crag Foot chimney, all backed by the Bowland moors featuring Ward's Stone and Clougha Pike.* A thinner path heads off, gently down and along the bottom of this scrubby tract to a path crossroads at the end of the embank-ment at the foot of Heald Brow. *This is a crossroads with WALK 8.*

Advancing straight on between outflowing stream and scrubby bank, the path leads to the landmark chimney at Brown's Houses. *This survives from a copper-smelting mill that once operated here, the original one in Elizabethan times. Note the bizarre collapsed concrete bridge over the channel. The isolated Brown's Houses are the clue to an easy walk into Silverdale, by way of the narrow road that serves the cottage. Part way along a stile on the left invites you into the National Trust-owned promontory of Jack Scout, where a labyrinth of paths lead through scrub and open limestone pasture, ultimately reaching a restored limekiln behind which a kissing-gate leads back onto the lane.*

Most rewarding continuation, if conditions permit, is the coast option. The route is clear, though the variation will depend on the state of the tide. If favourable, remain on the beach side of the craggy foreshore, around Jack Scout. Around Jenny Brown's Point a stone embankment extends out into the water. *This was part of a failed 19th century land reclamation scheme. A little stone jetty was a berth for boats linked with the smelt mill.* A little further are more substantial crags, this habitat of climbers is also known as Cow Mouth. Beyond this small 'inlet' a path largely traces the grassy brow above the cliffs and alongside enclosed farmland. With only an occasional deviation to beach level, the well-tramped path advances around Know End Point to reveal Silverdale's beach. The village centre is up the road accessing the beach. *Here two hotels, the Silverdale and the Royal, offer refreshment, along with a Post office, shops, WC, and a fine Millennium clock.*

Much easier walking on turf leads along to the front, where cars are often parked. An intense grassy covering now takes over, a bridleway route crossing to a prominent inlet at The Cove. Equally prominent is a cave in the wallside ahead. Turn up into this hollow to the base of the access road, which rises onto the through road. Turn right, and very soon a verge path starts on the left and runs to a stile at the start of a snicket. This enclosed way leads between houses and out onto Wallings Lane. Advance briefly along, then keep straight on the access road ahead. This ends in a garden where take a small gate ahead to resume along another snicket. Quickly absorbing another drive this runs on to the top of Elmslack Lane. Here turn left (Castle Bank) into a corner of the delightful Eaves Wood.

Turn sharp right on the main path along the base of the wood. After a short spell enclosed by walls the path runs more freely on, and will lead unfailingly back towards the start. For an interesting variation take a fork left soon after the wall there ends, and rise to a higher, parallel path. Turn right on this, and at an early fork keep left. Rising slightly, this runs on to arrive plum in the centre of a ring of beeches. *Some 17 strides in diameter, this stately circle dates from Victorian times.* The path continues to a junction in front of a forlorn ruin. Turn right to start descending, soon forking right again to descend more steeply to pick up the wood bottom path again. Go left to an early junction, then turn sharp right and this grand path runs on through tapering woodland to return to the car park.

Old smelt mill chimney, Brown's Houses

31

7

TROWBARROW

START Leighton Moss   Grid ref. SD 477750

DISTANCE 5^{1}2 miles (9km)

ORDNANCE SURVEY MAPS
1:50,000
Landranger 97 - Kendal & Morecambe
1:25,000
Explorer OL7 - English Lakes South East

ACCESS Start from Storrs Lane, east of the Leighton Moss visitor centre at Myers Farm. Roadside parking. RSPB car park for bona fide reserve visitors only. Silverdale rail station close by. Served by bus linking Silverdale village and station.

> *A variety of absorbing features are discovered within a stone's throw of a famous bird reserve*

Leighton Moss is a popular Royal Society for the Protection of Birds reserve best known for its elusive bitterns, with their strange 'booming' call, while rare avocets and marsh harriers might also be seen here. Originally a tidal inlet, by the mid 19th century the moss had silted up such that it was only flooded by high spring tides. At the end of the 19th century century drainage took place with the construction of floodbanks, dykes, and a pump house. Although highly productive, drainage ceased in the 1910s, and the re-flooded moss again became a wildlife haven of shallow meres and reedbeds. The moss came into the RSPB's care in the 1960s. There is a shop and tea-room at the visitor centre.

A short way east along Storrs Lane from the RSPB entrance take a kissing-gate on the left, from where two paths depart. Choose the permissive one which runs along the wallside. Keep on at a crossroads in the trees, and through a trough a memorial gate gives access to Trowbarrow nature reserve - 'The Trough' on maps. A well-made path leads into the heart of the site, where swinging left quickly reveals the immense scale of the old quarry. *A massive limestone cliff awaits, proving a classic switch from industry to leisure, as this has become a hugely popular climbing venue.*

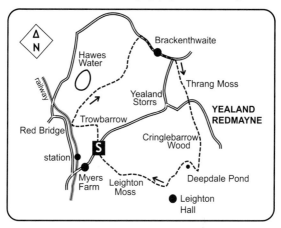

The quarry operated for around a century up until the 1950s, and was best known for pioneering a new 'tarmacadam' process, where crushed limestone was mixed with hot tar. The resulting 'Quarrite' was used to surface Blackpool Promenade a century ago. From the massive 'Shelter Stone' in the centre, turn left on a broad carriageway out of the quarry area. This runs on through a sliver of woodland and winds down to the site of Trowbarrow Limeworks. *Here an enormous Hoffman Kiln operated in the latter half of the 19th century: to appreciate the scale of this industrial edifice visit the surviving Hoffman Kiln not too far away at Langcliffe, near Settle in the Yorkshire Dales.* Just beyond, it emerges onto a back road at Red Bridge.

Turn right on the road, and after a row of houses take a gap-stile on the right. Squeeze past a barn and angle gently away from the road, a clear path forming as a wooded bank is scaled near the end. The path rises to a gap-stile into trees then on through limestone woodland to meet a wall. Here it swings right to a stile out of the trees. Remain with the wall that swings round to run along a fieldside as far as a path crossroads. Ignore the gate/stile and advance to a gap-stile in the wall just ahead, in front of woodland.

Turn right along an enclosed green way. At the end it rises away from the wall a few yards to a junction: go left on the main track, which runs to the edge of the wood and then beyond a gate continues away as a fine enclosed cart track. Ignore any lesser branches right, and at the end the way runs on into open pastures, now as a mercurial green way. *Big open views reveal Farleton Fell and Hutton Roof Crags ahead, beyond dense woodland.* The way drops gently down through the fields to join a road. Turn right as far as a junction. *En route you pass Brackenthwaite Farm and New House Farm together, one with an impressively preserved limekiln, the other a fine pictorial sign.*

At the junction beyond, drop left a few yards and take a stile on the right. A vague path drops down a scrubby bank, fading as you head on to the edge of the walled wood on the right. Through the gap (exploited by a telegraph line), don't be tempted to remain with the wall on the right, but drop left past a pole to skirt the right side of Thrang Moss to a corner stile and bridge on a drain. Bear right on the drain-side track, rising out of the birchwood into a field. Ascend with the fence to a gate onto a road. *There is a glimpse of Ingleborough from the top of the field.*

Cross straight over to a stile, and a delightful path runs through the strip of woodland to merge into a broader green way. This rises through plantings to a gate into the more natural Cringlebarrow Wood. Rising gently past low limestone outcrops, the broad path reaches an island pasture. Though slanting right across its corner, a permissive path turns right to remain on the wood edge. Along the other side the path heads back into trees, slanting up through a limestone scar to meet a broader track. Detour right here, briefly, then off left on a thin path which quickly rises onto Cringlebarrow's small open area at Round Top. *This provides views north-west to Arnside Knott, and the Lakeland Fells beyond the estuary.*

The main route turns left on the broad track, running just beneath Cringlebarrow's modest ridge top then gently down to a path junction. Keep straight on, still gently down to merge into a broader path. Just beyond is a gate/stile out of the wood.

However, through it turn sharp right to a stile fronting a small lime-stone scar, beyond which a path drop through trees to a small gate, then slants down through dense scrub above the deep bowl of Deep Dale. The path angles down and doubles back beneath a limestone bluff for a short, steep drop into the bowl, where Deepdale Pond awaits. *This is emphatically a surprise, a round scoop of water in this remarkably deep hollow, awash with springtime bluebells yet at other times almost sombre.*

The path circles to the far side and rises to meet a broader path. Turn left as this winds on through the trees, your path branching off the track to drop right to a gate on the edge of Leighton Hall parkland. *This earns immediate view over Leighton Moss to more distant scenes.* Bear left through another gate then down across the field centre to pick up a track towards Home Farm. A gate admits onto the access road. Your way is right, return-ing via Grisedale Farm to the track back across the moss. *Leighton Hall itself is two minutes to the left (visited in WALK 8).* Your way is right, down the surfaced access road to Grisedale Farm. Remain on the broad descending track, keeping right at a fork to run on to enter Leighton Moss. The hard track runs as a causeway across the centre, passing a public bird hide before reaching the road.

Leighton Moss

LEIGHTON HALL & MOSS

START *Silverdale   Grid ref. SD 476751*

DISTANCE *6 miles (9$\frac{1}{2}$km)*

ORDNANCE SURVEY MAPS
1:50,000
Landranger 97 - Kendal & Morecambe
1:25,000
Explorer OL7 - English Lakes South East

ACCESS *Start from Silverdale rail station. Limited roadside parking, further parking near the RSPB Leighton Moss visitor centre on Storrs Lane just over the rail bridge. Served by bus linking village and station.*

Easy walking through parkland and woodland either side of a famous bird reserve, along with coastal marshes and views

For a note on Leighton Moss see page 32. From the station walk south to the junction, then left on Storrs Lane over the rail bridge and past the visitor centre. Turn off right at the first chance along a broad causeway across the moss. Part way along is a public hide. At the end the track enters a field to climb to Grisedale Farm, above which its access road ascends to the farm buildings at Home Farm. Just a little further, a cattle-grid is crossed and Leighton Hall appears immediately on the right. *This imposing house was built in the latter half of the 18th century of local limestone in a truly beautiful setting. It is open to visitors, along with its grounds and gardens including a 19th century walled garden. There is a tea-room and a bird of prey collection, while numerous special events are held throughout the year.*

The footpath ignores the driveway in front, and turns to climb steeply alongside power lines. Past a fenced enclosure slant right to a pair of seats, an ideal break to look west over the hall and a beautiful backdrop beyond Leighton Moss. Resuming, ignore the main path south along the crest of the hill, and take a kissing-gate behind into the field there. Cross straight over to a very prominent mound, an ancient burial cairn. Behind it the path winds steeply down to a stile onto a lane climbing out of Yealand Conyers. *This delightful limestone village is a twin of the neighbouring Yealand Redmayne (see WALK 9).*

Turn up the road, and ignoring a path off to the right at a sharp bend, advance on from the bend a short way further and take a path branching off to the left. This runs on above the walled grounds of Yealand House, to a crossroads with an ascending path at the end of the wall. Bear right along this, crossing delectable limestone surrounds and on past a surviving limekiln. On past this a hedge leads out onto Peter Lane.

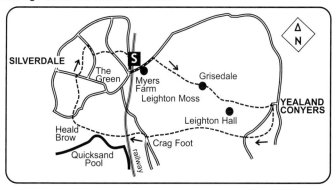

Cross straight over and along a cart track, for some time until a private sign interrupts. Here the path turns down to a stile in the wall below, and down a wooded bank. Cross the grassy shelf at the bottom and then bear left down the large open pasture, to a gate/stile at the foot of the wall. A grassy track forms to run on a field bottom, at the end of which a firm, broad track drops down a gap between woodland. *Looking ahead reveals the extent of Leighton Moss's marshes and pools.* Bearing left across the field to re-enter woodland, a path immediately branches off on a better way through the wood to rejoin the track at the end, there descending to a cluster of buildings and onto the road alongside a four-square chimney at Crag Foot. *This survives from a pump-house built to aid drainage of Leighton Moss in the late 19th century.*

Turn right on the road, with a useful footway for a few minutes until a rough lane branches left alongside the sizeable outflow from Leighton Moss. Beneath the rail bridge is a car park on the left for the bird hides, while your way branches right on a stone-arched bridge over the drain. Go left on the embankment which shadows the drain a short way then bears off right, a fine walk by Quicksand Pool to the base of Heald Brow. *En route the old chimney at Brown's Houses is prominent.* A stile admits to a path junction under the slope. Along to the left is Jenny Brown's Point, visited on WALK 6, but your route gets to grips with Heald Brow.

Turn right through the gateway and take the path ascending the scrubby slopes, winding steeply but pleasantly up. Be sure to look back for a splendid view over the embankment. A squeezer-stile/wicket-gate admit to the National Trust's more wooded Heald Brow, the path easing out as it swings a little left. Keep left at a fork, through the top edge of the trees to emerge with a wall-stile just ahead. Through it resume with the wall on your left through a couple of fields. *This stage offers glimpses of the Lakeland Fells beyond Arnside Knott.* At the end a bridle-gate sends a splendid hedgerowed path off to the right to emerge onto a road.

Just to the right a stile sends a woodland path off, at once forking. The left branch descends stone steps to run grandly on the wood edge. In the trees to your right is the limestone crag of Woodwell Cliff. A stile at the end puts you back into trees. On your right is the well itself. *This marks a substantial end to the cliff, and at the base of the rocks water drips dramatically out of the very crag into a stone trough. In front a reedy pond collects the water, with a long stone trough just across.* Take the continuing path straight on into trees from the pond's right corner. Almost at once it reaches the base of a further clean-lined cliff, and this you must climb! Panic not, it's really a natural staircase, but fun.

At the top resume left on the clifftop path for just 40 yards, then bear right on a path running to join a broader one. Turning left this takes a kissing-gate out of the trees, then bears more faintly right along the side of this island pasture. Up a low bank between trees it enters a higher-level pasture, going left to a kissing-gate back into trees. A grand path runs on to a corner stile out of the wood. It runs right along a fieldside outside houses, becoming a broad enclosed way to run out onto a road at Silverdale Green.

Turn right, then very quickly left along a small back road, The Green. Follow this as it winds around to the right (past Crinkle Cottage of 1552) through the heart of The Green (Silverdale Green) and out at the other end onto a road. Turn very briefly left before forking right on a cart track to Burtonwell Cottage. Keep straight on past it into the edge of a wood, a broad path running on then swinging left at the end, deep into trees. The path drops gently down to a kissing-gate at the end into Lambert's Meadow alongside Burton Well. Here a spring emerges into a vast, stone chamber.

Into the meadow a path heads away with the emerging stream. *The National Trust's Lambert's Meadow is a preserved island of green, damp meadow.* Reaching a footbridge, cross to a small gate across the field. Back into woodland a good path rises left, then runs on to emerge on the brow of a road. Turn briefly right then take a kissing-gate on the left onto enviably sited Silverdale golf course. Large yellow discs confirm the route which descends across a fairway, down a bank and across another, then down at the end to a stile onto Red Bridge Lane. Turn right to the station.

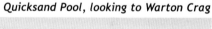

Quicksand Pool, looking to Warton Crag

AROUND TEWITFIELD

START *Tewitfield*   *Grid ref. SD 519736*

DISTANCE *7¹4 miles (11¹2km)*

ORDNANCE SURVEY MAPS
1:50,000
Landranger 97 - Kendal & Morecambe
1:25,000
Explorer OL7 - English Lakes South East

ACCESS *Start from Tewitfield Locks car park by the Longlands Hotel, where the A6070 Carnforth-Burton road bridges the M6. Carnforth rail station is a mile off-route.*

> *Hugely varied walking links attractive villages by way of canal towpath, fieldpaths, riverbank, and numerous historic features*

Tewitfield's flight of redundant locks on the Lancaster Canal are the only ones along its entire length. Construction of the M6 motorway in 1968 played havoc with the hapless canal, leaving Tewitfield the northern limit of navigation. Its eight locks remain in place, but minus their gates. The waterway from Preston opened in 1797, though it was a further 22 years before Kendal was reached. Its main role was to transport goods such as quarried lime south for agriculture, and coal northwards for industry. The canal company was taken over by the London & North Western Railway in 1864, a regular occurrence for waterways losing out to the far more efficient railways. The last coal barge ran in 1947.

From the end of the car park follow the short access road to discover the northern limit of the navigable canal at Tewitfield Basin. Turn right under the road bridge to find the start of the Northern Reaches, the severely fractured section of the canal that once ran to Kendal. *A long-term scheme to restore the waterway is in place.* Head north along the towpath with the less endearing company of the motorway on the other side - though increasingly screened. All eight old locks are passed, along with a stone-arched bridge and an old canal milestone on the opposite bank. *At the top a set of old lock gates stand forlornly on the grass. Views back look to the Bowland heights of Ward's Stone and Clougha Pike.*

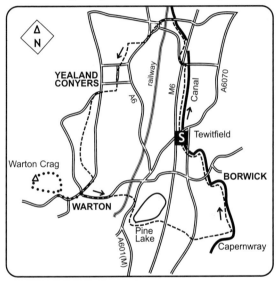

Just beyond, approaching Saltermire Bridge, take a gate/stile on the left where a section of old road leads you to a road by the bridge. Turn left over the motorway and a short way down the other side the canal reforms. An old iron kissing-gate puts you back on the towpath, and resume along here to climb steps onto the road at Yealand Road Bridge. Turn left to bridge the West Coast main line. *A wide range of Lakeland Fells is now on offer.* With a crossroads with the A6 in view ahead, turn left on a side road and follow this to join the A6: scattered ahead is the village of Yealand Conyers. Cross with care, ignore a stile and follow the verge for a couple of minutes to a gate on the right. Angle away from the road to a stile in a hedge, and resume towards Yealand Conyers by another intervening stile and along to a corner gate onto a road.

Turn right, and if heading for the inviting New Inn, follow it up to the main street, where you would turn left to rejoin the main route. Otherwise, at a crossroads turn left on Church Lane. This runs past St John's church and along to a junction. *Ingleborough raises its ever-graceful profile beyond Farleton Fell and Hutton Roof Crags.* Cross straight over and along a driveway to the houses at Dykes House. Keep on to the end where a small gate puts you into a field. Ascend directly to a wall-stile at the top. *Views back embrace some Lakeland Fells as well as Great Coum and Gragareth on the edge of the Dales.* Turn left along the road to a T-junction. *Alongside is a Friends' Meeting House of 1692 in a typically secluded Quaker burial ground. Mounting steps stand on the road outside.*

Turn right up the steep Peter Lane, and levelling out along to the left take a stile on the left. Through a few trees the path emerges into a long, open pasture beneath low limestone outcrops. This runs a delectable course to the far end, where a stile admits into the Woodland Trust's Hyning Scout Wood. Three paths head away: take the central one running a splendid course above a limestone scar. It drops slightly to a junction with a path coming up from the left. Bear right along it, and just a little further take a thinner branch left. This drops down, merging with another from the right to reach a crossroads. The right branch quickly runs to a wall-stile onto a cart track. Turn left on here to join the road.

Part way along you pass a restored limekiln. Turn right on the road into Warton. *Wrapped in suburbia, its pleasant centre features pub and church. The George Washington recalls the village's links with the US president, whose family lived here in the 15th century. The church of St Oswald has an imposing 15th century tower, and across the road is the Old Rectory, a substantial 700-year old ruin in the care of English Heritage. The village has a Post office/shop, WC and 17th century dated lintels on numerous houses.* • *Worth a memorable short hour's detour is Warton Crag - see overleaf.*

The main route departs left on Borwick Lane before the village centre. Passing a modern Methodist church, a parallel street on the right offers escape from traffic, rejoining the lane at the end and continuing to a farm on a bend. Turn right down the track between the buildings, a pleasant enclosed course to pass beneath the West

Coast main line and along to the A6. Safely across, a small gate sends a path right outside Pine Lake resort to emerge onto a busy roundabout. Crossing the resort access road the path resumes inside its boundary fence. At a corner it swings left to trace the River Keer upstream outside the resort. Simply remain on the beck's bank all the way - with views across the lake - to finally leave the site and utilize a concrete walkway under the motorway. Continue past another lake to wind around to Kellet Lane as it bridges the Keer at High Keer Bridge.

Cross the bridge and resume on the other bank, this time in the adjacent fields. In the third one cut a corner of the beck and advance to a gate in front of the Keer Viaduct. *This carries the Carnforth-Skipton railway line over the young river.* Pass under the arches and up the field to a corner stile onto a lane at Capernwray. Go briefly left and at the bridge join the towpath of the canal. Follow this north and it will lead unfailingly back to the start. *At once you cross the splendid single-span Keer Aqueduct: opened in 1797, it carries the waterway 35ft over the Keer. Behind it you pass under the Skipton line, past some moorings, and a tiny arm that served a limestone quarry.*

Borwick Hall

WALK 9 • AROUND TEWITFIELD

Emerging you pass another old milestone. The second of two road bridges is reached at the western edge of Borwick village. Borwick Hall can be glimpsed from the towpath, but by crossing the bridge it is but a minute's walk for a closer inspection. This magnificent building incorporates a 14th century pele tower and an Elizabethan great hall. The gatehouse through which you might glimpse the grandeur bears a 1650 datestone. Rejoin the towpath to trace its final curves back to the start. En route you pass another milestone and Tewitfield Methodist Church, still in service.

• WARTON CRAG

Head along Crag Road from the pub, and at the car park follow a path up beneath a quarried wall to reach a wall-gap onto another path. Entering Warton Crag nature reserve, turn right up the path through a kissing-gate onto the bottom corner of the fell, where the path splits. Take the left branch which slants up a natural line by low limestone terraces and scrub. *Views rapidly open out from Ingleborough around to the Bowland moors, with Carnforth below and Morecambe Bay outspread beyond.*

Maintain this steady rise to reach a gate above a massive old quarry. Leaving the nature reserve, a path heads away outside the quarry fence, but within thirty yards take a branch right which rises directly through low limestone terraces to the base of a larger cliff. A stile sees the path make an easy passage between the rocks, then rising just the short way further to arrive at limestone outcrops that form a superb viewpoint on the Beacon. The beacon itself and OS column occupy the summit of Warton Crag at 534ft/163m just behind. *Highlight of the view is the prospect over the bay, from nearby saltmarshes to Grange-over-Sands, Jenny Brown's Point, Middlebarrow and Silverdale, beyond which rises a long skyline of Lakeland Fells from Black Combe to Fairfield.*

Behind the beacon is a guidepost as the path forks. Take the right one, which runs a grand course on a gentle slant down through trees. At a major fork bear right through an old wall and then down, through a breach in the limestone and superbly down through trees to meet a path at the bottom edge of the wood. Turn right on this to return to the kissing-gate near the start, and back down to the car park.

10

CLAWTHORPE FELL

START Holme   Grid ref. SD 524788

DISTANCE $4^3/4$ miles ($7^1/2$km)

ORDNANCE SURVEY MAPS
1:50,000
Landranger 97 - Kendal & Morecambe
1:25,000
Explorer OL7 - English Lakes South East

ACCESS Start from the village centre. Roadside parking. Served by Lancaster-Kendal bus.

> *A magnificently varied walk featuring limestone nature reserve and canal towpath between neighbouring villages*

Holme is a pleasant linear, grey-stone village with its nucleus around the church of the Holy Trinity, close by which are the Smithy Inn, Post office and shop. The Lancaster Canal runs parallel, forming an effective moat to keep the similarly parallel motorway at bay. From the church turn north along the street, and gain the canal towpath by turning right up a lane immediately before the school. This runs on to serve sports fields: as it rises to bridge the canal, a path forks left outside the school field to join the bank.

Follow the towpath right along the edge of the village, passing the site of Holme Coke Ovens on the opposite bank. *Barely discernable is a dark hole in the undergrowth, all that remains of a bank of five ovens. Built some time after the opening of the canal in 1819, when coal would be transported here to be part burned to produce coke. This would then be carried off again and used as a fuel for iron smelting. Unfortunately its lifespan was cut short when the railways replaced the slower pace of the canal system.*

Just a little further is Sheernest, where cottages and bridge form an attractive scene. Resume south along the towpath's delightful course for almost a mile further. *En route is much to enjoy: almost at once you have big views to the richly-wooded AONB area backed by the South Lakeland fells; contrastingly closer is Holme Mills, whose pond makes a nice foreground. Hard to imagine that hundreds were employed here in the 19th century, while the canal saw endless activity as packet boats took goods to Lancaster. The canal is carried over a road on an aqueduct encased in foliage: the Dutton Arms pub is glimpsed down to the right.*

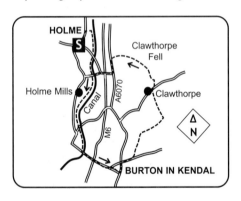

A little after Burton village appears across the motorway, leave the towpath on a broad stepped path doubling sharply back down to the right onto Station Lane. Turn under the aqueduct, up the road over the motorway to the village edge. At the fork, go right for the centre. At the fork an old Westmorland County Council sign still points to the long closed station. *Twin of neighbouring Holme, Burton in Kendal is a splendid village astride the old Lancaster to Kendal coaching route. The Kings Arms and the Royal Hotel survive from those days, while handsome 18th century houses, some with overhanging balconies, stand back from the Market Square. Close by the 18th century market cross are the picturesque cottages of Cocking Yard. The Manor House has a 1701 datestone. Burton has a Post office/shop, while the old church of St James with its squat tower stands at the northern limit of the village.*

Head north along the main street past the school and village hall to a crossroads, and take Vicarage Lane rising right. Climbing away, quickly turn left at a grassy gap between hedges on the left between houses. This is Slape Lane, which swings right behind a house wall and heads away between hedgerows to remain a classic tramp for a considerable time. *There are odd glimpse across the fields to the Beetham area and a distant skyline of Lakeland fells.*

Gaining a little height, woodland comes in on the left and the way rises to a junction with a firm track. Abandon your lane and turn left through the gate. This track runs pleasantly through a narrow enclosure, largely surrounded by woodland to approach Oakwood Farm at Clawthorpe. *En route you pass a large, well-preserved limekiln.* A succession of gates leads through the farm, crossing the yard at the end to a small gate out onto a minor road.

Turn right, ignoring an immediate turn left along a back lane, and continue up to the end of the few houses, where a woodland track turns off left alongside Holme Park Quarry nature reserve. Don't enter the reserve, on the right, but head away along the straight, level track through the trees. At the end it emerges into a clearing on Clawthorpe Fell. *Entering this National Nature Reserve is a super moment as you are faced with a spectacular, tilted limestone pavement featuring some weirdly square blocks. Rare flowers survive in the few grikes (gaps in the limestone, where shrubs and small trees also attempt to gain a foothold).*

The path is immediately faint: bear gently left on a level course over the slabs to a wall at the far side. Turn down this and a clearer path reforms at the corner, through a little limestone and undergrowth to a stile in the wall. The path heads away outside the limits of the working quarry, soon dropping left to descend more directly though woodland. At the bottom a gate admits into a field corner. Look back to the left to see a fine limekiln at the field top, then descend your fieldside to a gate/stile back onto the A6070.

Go left for no more than five minutes to the junction of the Holme road (B6384). Turn right here, immediately bridging the M6 to drop towards Holme. As it swings right to the edge of the village, turn left down narrow Sheernest Lane to the canal bridge. Across, turn down steps on the left to gain the grassy towpath. Here you rejoin the outward route to retrace steps back into the centre of Holme.

FARLETON FELL

START Crooklands   Grid ref. SD 540821

DISTANCE 6 miles (9¹2km)

ORDNANCE SURVEY MAPS
1:50,000
Landranger 97 - Kendal & Morecambe
1:25,000
Explorer OL7 - English Lakes South East

ACCESS Start from Moss Side just along the A65 Skipton road from the A65/A590/A6070 roundabout by Junction 36 of the M6. Lay-by alongside Lancaster Canal. Served by Kendal-Ingleton bus.
• OPEN ACCESS - see page 6.

> *A rewarding exploration of stunning limestone scenery,*
> *concluding on a lovely section of canal towpath*

Farleton Fell is most prominent of several names given to the highly individual upland tract overlooking Junction 36 of the M6. Other sections, both explored on this walk, are Newbiggin Crags and Holme Park Fell. The hill is dominated by delectable limestone scenery, featuring pavements and crags, escarpments and boulders. Leave the lay-by at a gate/stile into a field alongside the cafe, and descend to a stile at the bottom. Advance along the hedge to a gate, just past which a short track runs to Dove House Farm. Turn right on the access road, quickly reaching a junction where turn left on a grassy lane that meanders down to meet Lupton Beck at stone-arched Nook Bridge. *Across is a curious little verge garden.*

Across the bridge take a gate on the left, pass through the central gate behind and bear left across the field to slant up a gap in the low wooded bank. Down to your left a steep wooded bank drops to the beck. Entering a large sloping field keep left above the beck, and part way along turn up the field centre beyond a solitary oak, rising to a stile at the top. *Look back for extensive views to the Lakeland Fells.* Continue on with a hedge, revealing Aikbank Farm beneath the colourful slopes of Farleton Fell. Drop down through a stile to a gate into the house environs. Descend to another and out on the drive onto Puddle Mire. At the bend of a surfaced road turn right up it to a T-junction with Puddlemire Lane.

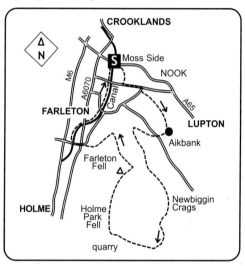

Cross straight over onto a cart track slanting right beneath dense gorse along the base of the fell. Ignoring an early branch doubling back left, remain on the hedgeside to where a second branch does the same. Take this one, doubling sharply back up through still dense gorse, enjoying a sustained, gradual rise up the fellside. *The Lakeland Fells are seen beyond Junction 36, while closer to hand across the Lupton Valley are Great Coum, Gragareth and ever-graceful Ingleborough.* Suddenly and quite unexpectedly you emerge onto contrastingly grassy open fell. Several paths depart: go left, rising briefly onto a plateau where the main path swings right on a long slant up the open fell. Ignore this and take either of two thinner paths rising directly away. After a short pull you meet a broad green way running along a tilted shelf. Go left on this the short way to a gate in a wall. Note the massive natural gatepost. Pass through onto the edge of Newbiggin Crags.

Follow the main path only briefly, then take a thinner but clear branch right. This winds up the slope, doubles back up to meet the wall, then runs thinly on to a path junction at a wall junction. Don't pass through the gate on the right, but go left on another broad grassy way. This remains underfoot for a considerable time as it runs to a bend overlooking a magnificently colourful scene, the Newbiggin Crags area at its finest. *All this is foreground to a super backdrop stretching from the Howgill Fells to Ingleborough.*

Ignoring a branch dropping left into this area, remain on the main path as it runs to a crossroads leaving the rugged limestone environs behind. *Morecambe Bay appears, as does neighbouring Hutton Roof Crags, a contrastingly scrub-draped landscape.* Now take the clearer path forking right, soon merging with another from the right and dropping to negotiate a splendid limestone pavement and then down across grassland, becoming a firmer track. With a minor road in view just ahead, a crossroads with a bridleway is met just before telegraph poles. Here turn right to a bridle-gate. Cross the field centre to a gate ahead, from where a good track heads off through a tangle of open country. This descends and runs on to a gate onto the National Trust's Holme Park Fell.

At once the track forks: remain on the main one straight ahead, outside the boundary of Clawthorpe Quarry. *The Coniston Fells are prominent ahead.* Remain on this fell-edge track alongside splendid limestone scenery, dropping gently towards a wall. *An old limekiln is seen down to the right.* Without passing through the gate, double back right on a more inviting track which begins a long, steady rise beneath the tilted scars of Holme Park Fell.

You can follow its leisurely course all the way to the top end, or ideally, make use of an early gap in the cliff and instead follow the edge on a sustained but very steady rise alongside tilted limestone pavements to ultimately gain the summit of the fell. *Throughout this stage savour views claiming a stunning variety of features including the Lakeland Fells, Morecambe Bay, the Lancaster Canal and the Bowland moors. Less endearing are the quarry behind you and the motorway far below.* Rounded boulders mark the high point at 869ft/265m. *This is all classic stuff, from the stunning limestone uplands alongside to the splendid distant views. These include Ingleborough and the rolling fells of the western Dales, in addition to Lakeland and the Bay.*

Leave by advancing to the wall just ahead, then following it briefly right to a stile in it. Here you trade Holme Park Fell for Farleton Fell. Meeting a path on its other side, double back left a short way then bear right over a little knoll and along the path to the distinctive landmark cairn on Farleton Knott.

The next stage demands a little caution to ensure you select the right way off the fell. Of various paths and trods departing, not all offer sensible routes. The best one uses a cairned ascent path from Farleton, but on leaving the top this is not initially evident. With the first cairn not immediately visible, leave by a little trod heading north, soon forking right on dropping from the knott's mound and crossing a broader green way. By now you can locate a marker cairn which is the first of many that guide an intricate route down the fellside. From sighting this cairn, plain sailing should ensue. A smaller cairn is seen lower down, and a thin path winds down by several more to approach the upper limit of the otherwise impenetrable gorse.

Below is a veritable bird's-eye view of the Farleton area. Abundant cairns guide a clear little path down through the gorse, to a point where it swings left to contour along for some time. The last stage is a much improved slant down an old quarrymens' way, passing beneath a massive scree slope to meet a lower path. Turn left along the base of the fell to soon reach a stile beneath a stand of trees. Descend the fieldside to a gate/stile onto the road at Townend Farm on the edge of Farleton.

Advance straight on to a crossroads with the A6070. Go straight across and over Duke's Bridge on the Lancaster Canal. Descend stone steps on the left and double back under the bridge to enjoy the final stage back to the start point. Simply follow this splendid towpath all the way back to the A65 at Moss Side. *En route you pass Farleton with colourful views of its fell receding, and pass under a number of quality bridges before a dead-straight spell, over an aqueduct on Farleton Beck and passing an old milepost.* Reaching the truncated end of the waterway ignore the pedestrian underpass and simply turn up past the canal end to re-enter the lay-by.

HUTTON ROOF CRAGS

START Lupton   Grid ref. SD 554811

DISTANCE 5^{1}2 miles (9km)

ORDNANCE SURVEY MAPS
1:50,000
Landranger 97 - Kendal & Morecambe
1:25,000
Explorer OL7 - English Lakes South East

ACCESS Start from the A65, roadside lay-bys opposite the Plough.
Served by Kendal-Ingleton bus. • OPEN ACCESS - see page 6.

An absorbing landscape of limestone outcrops with big views

Hutton Roof Crags is a delectable upland dome dominated by limestone outcrops of crags, pavements, scars and boulders, enriched by the colour of dense gorse vegetation. Not visited on this walk, the high point is a modest 899ft/274m, its trig point not shown on all maps. Be warned, there is far more to this place than the map suggests! Lupton is little more than its pub, the Plough, and a handful of houses on the busy A65 from West Yorkshire to the M6 and the Lake District. Up a back road is All Saints church.

Just south of the Plough follow the grass verge to Dorothy Wightman Interiors and into the car park, then out the bottom and down a cart track. Facing you are the colourful flanks of Farleton Fell, while your goal of Hutton Roof Crags is set insignificantly back to the left. The track descends, ultimately steeply, to a ford and footbridge on Lupton Beck. You only cross this at the end of the walk, so for now turn left across the field to a ruined farm. From a gate in the wall alongside cross to a stile in the far corner, and from one behind trace a little green way slanting left up the low bank. Head away along the fieldside with a little stream on your left.

Towards the end cross a fence-stile and resume on the other side. To the left is Lupton Tower. *The western section is a defensive pele tower dating back around 500 years.* From a stile at the end rise up the field centre to a squeezer-stile. *Look back to see an array of Lakeland Fells.* Cross to the right side of the houses ahead, where a stile puts you onto a narrow lane. Go left to a junction just short of the A65, and turn right past the old farm at Green Lane End.

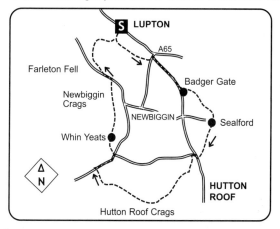

The back road drops down between hedgerows past Lupton Mill to Lupton Bridge. *This lovely corner at the old mill features a pond and charming woodland.* Crossing the arched bridge take a stile on the left beneath Badger Gate farm, and cross to a gate just ahead. Advance briefly on a track, but then cross the field centre parallel with the beck, passing through a gate midway and on to a stile. Slant right up a reedy pasture to a corner stile, and head away with a fence on your left. *Here you enjoy good views to the nearby Dales fells across the Lune Valley.* Descending towards a pond, curve right to cross a stile and advance to Sealford Farm.

Joining Sealford Lane go right just a few strides and head away along an enclosed green way. Part way on take a gate on the right and ascend to a stile above. Now bear left over the brow to find a corner stile. *Looking back, Ingleborough is well seen.* From a ladder-stile just beyond, Hutton Roof church appears ahead. Go left to a

53

small gate into the environs of Pickle Farm. Follow the drive out only briefly, then take a gate on the left into a garden. Cross to a gate out of it and bear right along a limestone-scattered pasture towards the church, joining the road a little further left by means of a neat wall-stile. *The modest church of St John dates from 1881. Tiny Hutton Roof itself is a little further south along the road.*

Turn right to the junction and go briefly left. *Alongside the church is the former school of 1897.* Here take a stile on the left from where a well-tramped path rises across a field into under-growth, and then runs delightfully on through dense woodland. *Note the saturation coverage of lichen on the limestone boulders.* A stile at the other end admits you into the open country of Hutton Roof Crags. Advance a short way to join the right of way across the fell, just in front of an old limekiln. Turn right on the path to ascend by a wall to soon enter more open, better graded slopes, a lovely broad green rise. *Big views look back over the Lune Valley to the Middleton Fells leading the eye to the Howgill Fells.*

Part way up is a distinct fork. While the right of way goes straight on, instead take the left option which breaks through the little 'edge' and runs on to an early junction, where bear right. As this forks take the right one, slanting more gently up: the left option accesses The Rakes, a tilted line of crags descending away. *This is a very popular climbing area. Views have now opened out southwards to the Bowland moors beyond your own immediate and absorbing collection of limestone interspersed with scrub.* Your path rises to a little brow. *Farleton Fell is straight ahead now and the Lupton Valley below, with a glorious Dales skyline behind.* Advance towards Farleton Fell, along a distinct brow where fork left on a thinner path heading for a wall of crags just ahead.

Quickly meeting a path from the right, turn left on it parallel with the wall of limestone. At the end of the rocks this forks: take the left one straight ahead: this ambles around the left edge of higher ground, revealing the fell's high point some way ahead. The path rises gently up and along between superb tilted limestone pavements. Passing through a hollow, keep to the main path to the far end, on through trees and down into a larger clearing. Emerging through limestone at the other end, keep going through the scrub and trees of Potslacks, a delightful path. The path runs on to emerge, dropping gently down with a view ahead towards Morecambe Bay.

Uberash Plain presents an open area to the left beneath a band of limestone. The path forges straight on, descending a groove to suddenly emerge with stupendous views, swinging sharp right over open terrain to contour along towards Farleton Fell. Further, it drops into increasingly dense gorse, and a distinct fork. Turn sharp right, and within a minute it reveals a kissing-gate onto the minor road severing Hutton Roof Crags from neighbouring Farleton Fell.

Turn right to the brow, down to a crossroads, then left on the farm road to Whin Yeats. *Outstanding views look to the Howgill Fells, Middleton Fells, Great Coum and Ingleborough.* Entering the yard of this extensive farm, take a gate on the left before the end to enter open country. A track heads away through a gate and along the fell. As it swings up to the left, a waymark sends the bridleway branching right to slant down gorse slopes. At the bottom corner it drops down an enclosed way onto Puddlemire Lane at Town End, Newbiggin. Turn left on this peaceful back road beneath the steep flanks of the fell and looking over the Lupton Valley. Entering the bracken-covered open country of Puddle Mire, bear right on an inviting track which runs parallel, slowly swinging round to the right, down the common to meet a firmer track towards the bottom. This quickly joins the old road, a firm track descending through a gate off the common into a beckside pasture. Cross to the footbridge and ford on Lupton Beck and retrace opening steps up to Lupton.

Limestone pavement, Hutton Roof Crags

INDEX *(walk number refers)*

WALK LOG

WALK	DATE	NOTES
1		
2		
3		
4		
5		
6		
7		
8		
9		
10		
11		
12		